Eleanor Roosevelt

Eleanor Roosevelt

*A Face of Humanitarianism
and Social Change
1884-1962*

Crystal Roberts

To order additional copies of this book, contact:
Xlibris Corporation
1-888-795-4274
www.Xlibris.com
Orders@Xlibris.com
100844

Table of Contents

Introduction

The idea behind this book came from my senior thesis written for my Bachelor's degree in 2010. The amount of research here resulted in many hours of reading book after book, websites, and articles, coming to the conclusion that Eleanor Roosevelt became the most politically active humanitarian of her time.

Albeit, students from high school through the junior college may find this book interesting as it is resourceful and inspiring to those who want to follow in the footsteps of a great humanitarian and political activist, who believed in the rights of women, the elderly, children, immigrants, the disabled, our military soldiers and veterans.

Acknowledgements

I would like to thank several people to whom this book would not have been possible. For my mother Alta Roberts, her continued support and encouragement during the writing of my thesis and made the outcome of this book possible. Secondly, to Dr. Clements for his continued encouragement in the classroom at Brandman University and for the opportunity to work with him on writing the History of the Vietnam War textbook, 2010-2011. I will always be grateful for the inspiration he has given me to pursue my love for History as a career. Finally to the many friends who have given me support as I took this journey to write my first book and to the many wonderful people at Xlibris who helped make this book a reality.

Preface

No other person early in the Twentieth Century had more compassion toward society, humanity, education, and Human Rights, as Eleanor Roosevelt.

This book [paper] will cover the life of Eleanor Roosevelt from her early years, through the White House years, to the Jews and Israel, and finally the labor unions and the United Nations.

As a child, Eleanor had been reminded constantly about her looks and her mother would always call her by her nickname that she gave to her as a child; this certainly would be heartbreaking for a child who only wants love and affection (especially from the one person who never gave her such love).

Eleanor did not have many friends growing up and always wished that she was beautiful like everyone else; this had always made her ashamed to be who she was. This fear of not being attractive made her awkward, quiet, and solemn for many years. As her years progressed, her mother died from diphtheria in 1892, although there are conflicting sources as to how her mother died, when she was eight years old. Two years later, her father died from a fall; however, there are conflicting remarks as to whether he died from a fall, alcoholism or both.

After both her parents had died, Eleanor went on to live with her grandmother. Living with Grandma Hall and her unmarried aunts, gave her a sense of home and love. At fifteen, Eleanor was sent to a finishing school "in 1899" in London.[1] Now, she found the family that continuously gave what she lacked in her own home life, to have affection and attention. Her peers looked up to her and adored her; much like a big sister.[2] The headmistress of Allenswood School saw a remarkable woman inside of Eleanor and knew that she had a special talent for leadership (as you will see later on in the book). Madame Souvestre took Eleanor on her travels around Europe as a means to give her a sense of independence and to see the world as it really was. [3] The two of them traveled during her school vacations. [4]

The atmosphere at the school Eleanor attended for three years (1899-1902) was a starting point that was unprecedented in her later years. As she blossomed, her ideas, beliefs, values, and hard were starting to pay off. She had the attention and recognition she longed for and [classmates] would flock to her with their problems and worries. [5]

After spending three years at Allenswood, Eleanor went back to New York to Grandma Hall. [6] Eleanor had her society debut as a young woman of eligible marrying age (fall 1902). During the Victorian Era, young women had balls or fancy parties that introduced them to society when they came of age. Coming of age meant they were old enough to date and hopefully find a suitable man in the hopes of getting married and having a family of their own. At this time, Eleanor was still not sure of herself (in many respects) outside of the young woman she became at Allenswood School in London.

Now that she was back in New York, she started volunteering at shelters down on the East Side of New York. [7] In this place, huge amounts of people were homeless, out of jobs, and had no money to feed their families. [8] Many other people lived in squalor and extreme poverty with no sanitation. Eleanor knew she needed to be here and to help. Eleanor brought Franklin there to see what she was doing and why she was there. [9] He was stunned and appalled at the sights, sounds, smells, and horrors that these people were forced to live. [10]

Eleanor also made several new friends that would surely influence the rest of her life to come. [11] One of these three women, Loraine Hickok, would become quite close with Eleanor over the years. She found great solace with "Hick" as she called her, and intimacy in the way of great personal and emotional, not a physical connection, which she did not have with Franklin. [12]

Over the years, Eleanor and Franklin would work together on many new projects, which included the New Deal program that was supposed to help the people during the years of the Depression Era (1929-1942). [13] Not every person benefited from this, therefore, the emergence of this new problem of the New Deal that did not include African Americans, women, or the disabled. [14]

The Wiltwyke School for boys was as near and dear to her as anything was. [15] She had helped thousands of boys at this school ". . . to learn, gain responsibility, trust, and love, without reprimands and punishment."[16] She was particularly horrified and could not believe why such boys would turn to a life of crime.[17]

Another interesting part of her life was how she helped the soldiers during World War II. She had flown to "Australia, New Zealand, Guadalcanal, and seventeen other islands."[18] To have such physical stamina during her travels of the South Pacific is quite extraordinary. In 1939, "She saw approximately four hundred thousand soldiers."[19] She gave and extraordinary amount of her time to many soldiers who were severely injured and grossly disabled, that she would forever remember each one of them for the rest of her life.[20] During her trips, she always listened to whatever they had to say always; showing interest in each person she talked with. She was interested in them, where they came from and if they had families (wives, children, parents, or siblings).[21]

She believed in helping the disabled and the mentally ill in becoming independent to where they gained employment and could live on their own.[22] This chapter discusses an intriguing and formidable man who worked with Eleanor Roosevelt in helping the disabled to get a better education and gain employment.[23]

Eleanor did not believe in segregation and she regularly had many African American people that she personally knew to cone to the White House for tea.[24] Constantly criticized for her work on segregation for African Americans was never ending. One such instance was Marion Anderson; a well-established and noted contralto (opera singer) was denied the right to perform at Constitution Hall in Washington (1939).[25] When Eleanor head that Marion was denied the right to perform, she in turn "dropped out of the Daughters of the Revolution" group.[26]

During the Depression (1929-1942), Eleanor (the women) gave many people who were desperate for work to feed their families.[27] They would come to the White House to interview Eleanor, [the worked for newspapers] which gave them a job that paid them enough money at times to pay for food, bills, rent, or other every day needs for survival.

Through the toughness and brassy exterior of Eleanor Roosevelt, there was another campaign that she believed in whole-heartedly, that any person of Jewish descent or anyone wanting to go to Israel at any time and feel welcomed into that country.[28] Many of the people she referred to were the immigrants and refugees. The refugees were those who escaped Germany during a time when persecution of Jews ran rampant (1939-1945) and here in Israel, they were accepted.[29]

The idea behind forming Israel as a sate unto itself was to help the people of this country to spread peace, democracy, and equality to all people and throughout the Middle East.[30] This was, in a sense. To stop Communism from spreading, but furthermore, it was the generosity of Eleanor that gave her the willingness to understand poverty, suffering, and to change what most people considered social suicide. In this case, Eleanor helped the Jewish community from all lifestyles to have not just America to go to, but have their own homeland, a place of prosperity and acceptance of their religion.[31]

Eleanor joined the labor unions (1937-1962) hoping to get better working conditions for women, stopping child labor, getting increases for working wages, and getting working time reduced to eight hours a day.[32] She had her own newspaper column in the New York Times and one hundred and seventy-nine other newspapers (1935-1962), which became famous as she worked on this column six days a week, called "My Day."[33] Through her travels, interviews, and lectures, I was amazed at her accuracy in which she managed her time for all the work she was involved in.

After Franklin died (April 12, 1945), Eleanor had duties to perform. President Truman asked Eleanor to be a delegate to a new group called, the United Nations (1945).[34] Here, she would find her most challenging campaign to win the right for every person, regardless of where they are from, the right to be an equal citizen with the rights in every possible way. She truly believed that, for peace to happen worldwide there needed to be an acceptance of every person and in every way.[35] The recognition of differences and uniqueness that everyone brings would constitute a great world and nation.

The emotional side of this book [thesis] is unavoidable, for anyone who cares deeply about people and greatly affected by the horrors against humanity or the greatest gift of all, that is, the touch of one stranger helping another human being, regardless of age, gender, race, or class, and how it changes them. Learning about Eleanor and her life is a valuable resource to how America's democracy, economic, and social areas have come a long way since the early nineteen hundreds.

The topic was selected to write about her life and why her work was so important to the history of this nation and beyond. The amount of resources used in the research and formation of this book [paper] significantly contributed to the knowledge about Eleanor Roosevelt. Many of the resources used will be books written by Eleanor herself, her son Elliot Roosevelt, Jr., and her good friend Joseph P. Lash, among other contributors. Other sources on Eleanor Roosevelt can be found at the end of this book in the bibliography and notes. An appendix is included to show her life in pictures which brings more of her personality and a personal connection to the reading.

1

The Early Years

A Lonely and Unsatisfying Childhood

Anna Eleanor Roosevelt was born on October 11, 1884, to Anna Hall and Elliot Roosevelt, in New York City.[36] Although she was not a pretty baby, as she grew, her beauty came within. According to her son James on how his grandmother [Anna] felt about his mother Eleanor:

> "She was annoyed that the daughter she bore was not a beauty. She repeatedly reminded the child that she was plain, with the result that Eleanor retreated into a shell, a shy, sad, soul. Believing her old-fashioned, Anna nicknamed her 'Granny.'"[37]

From her book, *The Story of Eleanor Roosevelt*, it described how Anna [mother] saw Eleanor as a child: "A shy girl, Eleanor had an awkward walk and teeth that stuck out. Her mother believed that beauty and good manners were important. She was ashamed of Eleanor's looks and made her feel bad." [38]

Anna died when Eleanor was ten years old in December 1892[39] while her father had been away in another state getting clean from his dependence on alcohol.[40] After her mother died in December 1892 from diphtheria,[41] Eleanor was not affected in ways that one ought to have acted after the death of a parent. Tragedy would strike her world again in two years with the death of her father in 1894.[42] Eleanor had a wall around her heart for a good reason. Her mother [Anna] was not as congenial toward her as she was to her other siblings. To tell a child for many years just how ugly their appearance is, tends to weigh on the mind and spirit of the individual. Eleanor surely felt this for many years until she went to Allenswood School in England (1903).

> "Eleanor always wanted to be the woman her father wanted her to be. Elliot gave her the ideals that she tried to live up to all her life by presenting her with the picture of what he wanted her to be-noble, brave, studious, religious, loving, and good."[43]

For the most part, the society in which Eleanor grew up, was full of dances, socializing, coning out parties (coming of age to marry), and other events in which the rich are expected to do and appear at.[44] High society puts on 'coming out parties' for girls of marrying age. The expectation to marry for a young woman during the Victorian Era and start a family was the norm. However, her childhood was a lonely, unsatisfying world where memories haunted her for the rest of her life.

The early life of Eleanor Roosevelt was traumatic if not downright daunting. She experienced the death of both parents and a sibling, living with her grandma Hall, several of her aunts, and uncles who were not exactly role models, shows that even high society has its share of family problems.

London, Allenswood, and Mlle. Souvestre

With the memories of her father and his letters that she always kept with her, she continually kept the close to her heart and read them often for comfort and support.[45]After a few weeks at the school, Eleanor started to loosen up a little and was soon making friends.[46] The girls had a rigorous schedule that they kept day and day out.[47] Eleanor was in a sense, the belle of the ball that she had always wanted to be. People loved and respected her, for Mlle. Souvestre had taught the girls that they must think for themselves.[48]

During her first year at Allenswood (1903), Eleanor flourished academically and socially. Her peers cherished her as a friend and classmate and her headmistress, Mlle. Souvestre took an interest in this shy, awkward, young woman.[49] Eleanor had never been interested in sports, which was for boys or men, not women.[50] However, she did excel in one particular sport and that was 'field hockey.'[51]

During Easter of 1901, Mlle. Souvestre took Eleanor with her on a trip to Italy and Paris, and here she was no longer within her familiarity or comfort zone and no companion to travel with her when she wanted to go and eat, shop, go to the movies, or even to the beach.[52] Mlle. Souvestre wanted Eleanor to go and explore the city on her own.[53] This was unheard of, but Eleanor languished in the thought of mingling with the many people, tasting the food, speaking the language, and experiencing the colorful culture of the Italian and French people. "She [Mlle. Souvestre] believed you should immerse yourself in the experience of another country, not only seeing local sights, but also eating indigenous foods and speaking native tongues."[54]

This opportunity gave her a sense of the lower classes which people were poor and middle classes who flourished. She started to learn that there is a whole world of people outside high society.[55]Analyzing the situation with Mlle. Souvestre says that she gave Eleanor a starting point in social work. Eleanor would cherish these travels with her headmistress and the two of them grew closer and closer each passing day, as if they were soul mates.[56]

Her headmistress was a lot of herself in Eleanor during her younger years and suspected that she would do exceptionally well in social work; more or less, she had hoped that Eleanor would be the same young woman after she returned home to New York.[57]

After three years at Allenswood (1899-1902), Eleanor returned to Grandma Hall in New York.[58] It was time that society met Eleanor as a young woman of marrying age (18). She was required to attend parties, dances, social events, among many things required of a young and wealthy girl.[59] She dreaded this, but knew that she could not hold out or say no to doing. Her early life was full of tragedy, disappointment, heartbreak, abuse, and one can clearly see, Eleanor was an orphan, as were the rest of her siblings. The family that she had longed for came from the most unexpected place on earth and that was the three years she spent at Allenswood School (1899-1902); the happiest Eleanor would ever be again.[60]

New York, Rivington Street, and the Women

After Eleanor returned to New York after leaving Allenswood in 1902, she began to give her time to people whom were less fortunate than she was. One of the places she started her volunteer work and her life long journey into the world of social work and social justice was at the Rivington Street Settlement (1903).[61]

Within this settlement, Eleanor began to see the one side of life away from high society, was sickening and horrifying for her. Here she met scores of people who got her interested in the social politics on the working conditions of men, women, and children. "After a brief introductory lecture in 'practical sociology,' they plunged into teaching calisthenics and dancing to a group of young East Side girls, although they had no previous training in how to manage children in groups."[62]

As Lash talks about the Rivington Settlements, he describes what the area looked like. In New York,

> "The Rivington Street Settlement two blocks south of Houston
> Street in one of the most densely populated parts of the city, was
> a harsh introduction in social realities. When the settlement was
> founded in 1889, the neighborhood had been German. Then it
> becomes predominantly Jewish; and now it was changing again
> as Italian emigrants flooded into the country."[63]

Lash also noted what kind of " . . . activities were practical-kindergartens for the young children, a gymnasium, classes in cooking, carpentry, art, and dancing, picnics in the woods and at the beach, and a summer camp in the country-and the settlement was also the center of a neighborhood effort for civic improvement."[64]

Her actual first taste of the lower and middle classes started when she helped her father and other people of her family do charity work. Lash gives a good explanation of what Eleanor did:

> "Until then Eleanor's contact with poor children had been
> slight: she had helped her father serve Thanksgiving dinner to
> the newsboys; she had assisted Uncle Vallie in decorating the
> Christmas tree for children in Hell's kitchen; and she had trailed
> along with her aunts to sing at the Bowery Mission . . . these
> activities had been charity, a continuation of the kind of work
> that had been started by her grandfather. Now she saw misery
> and exploitation on a scale she had not dreamed possible, and the
> pleas for legislative reform were more compelling to her because
> she saw the conditions to which they were addressed."[65]

The intensity, which Eleanor struggled to help overcome these obstacles of oppression for the immigrants that came to America, would dredge on for the rest of her life. Lash also noted about the Settlement's policies,[66] which Eleanor soon learned as a first lesson in the rights, which these people had and the work in which she was soon to be committed to, would fuel that desire to help people all over the world and the rights that all human beings are entitled to.

The next stage of her life dealt with Nancy Cook and Marion Dickerman, who all stayed close friends for many years. They had a place of their own called Val-Kill in Upstate New York that Franklin had built for them.[67] "Later on, Eleanor, Nancy, and Marion added a furniture workshop (1926) to the property and employed several local people in the manufacture of fine furniture."[68]

"Nancy Cook built some of the furniture for the cottage and that grew into the establishment of a furniture factory on the premises with the idea of giving local employment to local boys wanting to learn a trade."[69] This was a great idea for people who could not read or write. That person could at least be able to get a hand-on-education in making furniture, which in turn gave them the necessary skills to get a job.[70]

In 1927, Eleanor, Nancy, and Marion bought the Todhunter School.[71] When they did this, it was for the benefit of the children who went there. "Most of her students were the daughters of wealthy New York families, just as she had been."[72] As Westervelt pointed out, " . . . Eleanor taught the girls to think for themselves and took them to settlement houses, tenements, and police line-ups so they could have a broader perspective on city governments and social problems."[73]

> "Eleanor's friends meant more to her than support, companionship, affection. When she wrote Marion in 1926 that is "new" for her to have anyone recognize and care when she had moods, she betrayed how hard arid had been her world of love and friendship before she had been liberated from Mama and Franklin. That was all changed now. She had discovered the joys of openness and self-disclosure that came with real intimacy."[74]

After Franklin won the election for the presidency, there was an air of sadness. However,

> "Eleanor did not see much of Marion and Nancy with whom she had shared the responsibility of the Todhunter School and the Val-Kill furniture factory, for the factory had been sold in 1937 and moved to East Park, and she stopped teaching at the at the New York School when she moved to the White House."[75]

From many weeks of research and readings, Eleanor was very dedicated in the education of all classes of society. She, like her mentor, Mlle. Souvestre, believed that their students should have opinions and ideas of their own. Keeping a busy schedule with teaching, her other work, the many friends she stayed in contact with, many will wonder how in the world Eleanor stayed so energetic and positive. A good balance of bookkeeping, communication, a colorful level of attitude and understanding took enormous strides on mental, emotional, and physical capabilities to accomplish what she has done.

2

The White House Years

Wiltwyke School for Boys

The Wiltwyke School for abused and neglected boys was among Eleanor's many interests in 1942 and would continue to be so until her death in 1962.[76] Although not she was not credited for 'founding' the school, she nevertheless helped to keep the school open when she hear in the beginning that it was in severe financial difficulty.[77] This difficulty almost forced the school to close due to lack of funds (1942).[78] The school depended primarily on donations to give these boys a place to live and learn.[79] The boys found the necessary emotional, psychological, and physical necessities that every human needs in order to survive and be successful in life. These 'necessities' were love, understanding, compassion, patience, and a need to feel that they belong.[80]

However, she did acknowledge the urgency needed to help children from all backgrounds, not just from the upper wealthy class. This includes education, teaching responsibility, keeping children out of trouble and hoping that excellent guidance and leadership would inspire the children to want a future that is most advantageous and fun.[81]

It did not matter to Eleanor what religion, ethnicity, disability, or if the boys were immigrants or refugees.[82] Many boys, who came from bad homes, had become delinquents or wards of the state, boys who were abused, homeless, or any condition that robbed them of the childhood that all children should have; Wiltwyke was there for them.[83]

Although this school was not pristine on the outside, inside it provided a solid education and attention [love] that mattered to Eleanor Roosevelt.

Dr. Papanek a psychologist who took over for the previous administrator at the school, found ways to help the boys without punishments, by making the students take responsibility for their own actions and accept the consequences for those actions.[84] No spanking, no beating, or yelling, continued as was done by the previous administrator.[85] Teaching the students hope, love, understanding, trust, responsibility, and a sense of belonging among their peers, the boys learned that life could be exciting.

The children of Wiltwyke did not come from good homes. One example from Hershnan, described by Dr. Papanek:

> "David, for instance was nine when he was sent to us for pushing a little girl of five from a tenement roof. We found out that his mother kept him tied to a bedpost all day while she was out working. If he had soiled himself by the time she got home, she whipped him. The judge sent Nate to us because he had set fire to the tenement in which he lived. He told us that his home was a single room which he shared with his mother. She worked as a prostitute. One of the men gave her a silk scarf and Nate tried to burn it in the closet. Nate arrived with his face completely scarred. The glassful of lye which his father wanted to throw at his mother landed on him when he tried to defend her. Do you think these children need more punishment?"[86]

Eleanor understood how many of these children felt. She was an orphan whose family was not exactly the ideal family and she felt the need to help the children at Wiltwyke. The feeling of knowing that each child felt a sense of identity is recognized by Eleanor: "There is a desperate need for identification and recognition as an individual all through life to people who, because of circumstances or some limitations in themselves, have not learned to feel they have developed as individuals or have been so accepted . . ."[87]

One example shows how much she cared for the boys of Wiltwyke, when she invited the boys to her home at Hyde Park in New York:

> "Mrs. Roosevelt would put on picnics at her residence at Hyde Park in New York, reading to them, having a magician come and perform for them was her way of letting the children know that they were wanted and loved."[88]

She trusted all the boys with everything she had. At one picnic, she told all the boys at the table, "I have two hundred knives and two hundred forks; I want them all back after dinner!"[89] All the boys said yes Ma'am and they stuck to their promise to give back all her silverware.[90]

Many did not come back years later for the dinners put on every year, as some went to prison and others died.[91] This is common for any person in society. Sometimes people become mixed up in the wrong crowd of people and for others they just made bad decisions. Some people find school too hard because they lack self-esteem or have learning problems that are undiagnosed; this leads them to think they are unintelligent and they end up making bad decisions. Nevertheless,

> "On Mrs. Roosevelt's 70th birthday (1954), Dr. Papanek and some of his boys paid her a surprise visit. They serenaded her with her favorite song "Beautiful Dreamer" and brought her represents which every single one of the Wiltwyke boys had made for her . . . four of Dr. Papanek's boys marched in carrying an enormous birthday card which all the boys at Wiltwyke had helped to make and had signed."[92]

To see how dedicated she was to the school and to the children,

> "Eleanor Roosevelt's trust and devotion to the Wiltwyke School for Boys proved justified in the years that followed. Only twenty percent of the "Alumni" got into further trouble with the law. The school made a deep impression on its students, and many returned for visits long after they had graduated."[93]

This school did wonderful things for these children whose backgrounds, from which they came, many went on to do great things and have wonderful careers. One of these children was Floyd Patterson.

> "For a boy like me, a Negro, for whom there had been a growing awareness of what a difference in color meant, the interracial activities, whites being treated the same as the colored with no preference at all, this was a tremendous awakening. All religions were represented among the boys, but none was treated better or worse than any of the others. That's what helped to bring me out of the shell in which I had been living and what had helped me to make friends finally."[94]

Not every child was so fortunate to have a great career in boxing as Floyd Patterson, nevertheless, Eleanor and the staff at Wiltwyke did as much as they could short of these children being their own flesh and blood. It must have been wonderful to see so many children learning and making friends while they were learning to deal with their problems in a positive manner. This school was a safe haven for so many abused and neglected children when there was no other place for them to go but the street. At least someone cared enough to pull them from such a horrible existence, so that they may have a decent chance to live life, as children should.[95]

Immigrants and Refugees

Many Immigrants and refugees in other countries were so desperate to leave their own country, had exhausted all their resources and consul, that writing a letter to Eleanor Roosevelt was their last hope.[96] Eleanor Roosevelt helped many families stay together by granting them visas to come to America when she could do something about their situation.[97] However, not everyone got the help; she tried her best to go through the proper channels in order to help them.

In the book, *A Woman of Quality*, Hershnan talked of several stories where Eleanor helped people. Two stories from Hershnan's book are re-told here to show how intriguing they are. These people were not just from America but also from every corner of the world. One such story was "a ninety year old couple who were stuck in Havana since July 1, 1941," Mrs. Eisner wrote to Mrs. Roosevelt for help.[98] Here is what she wrote:

> "Dear Mrs. Roosevelt, as one grandmother to another, I am asking your help. Here we sit idle, a short distance away from our six grandchildren. Our days are numbered and every hour counts. My husband is ninety, and I am eighty years old. What possible danger can we be to the United States? Why not let us spend our few remaining years, perhaps only months, with our family?"[99]

She did all that she could to help the many who desperately needed her help. Helen Priester explained her situation that led her to write a letter to Eleanor Roosevelt, asking for her help.[100] Helen went overseas to visit and entertain our soldiers; she found herself one day going into an orphanage to entertain the children.[101] There she meets a child who would one day become her adoptive daughter.[102]

> "Even though she adopted Elena, she could not take her child out of the country. She tried everything, including applying for an emergency visa."[103]

> When Eleanor received her letter, she tried and tried to help Helen get her child to America, by going through Congress: The Senate and the House of Representatives.[104] Eleanor wrote letters to the Senate and the House of Representatives several times, until one of the representatives to the house and or the Senate finally agreed to help Helen bring her daughter home to America.[105]

The influence and caring nature of Eleanor Roosevelt, helped many refugees and tried to give each individual the assistance they crucially needed.[106]

A Soldier and His Parents

Eleanor Roosevelt has always been a woman who cared too much. When she decided to help someone, she not only considered his or her problem and situation, she did the impossible and made it possible in a short amount of time. One act of humanitarian kindness was when she helped a young German born Jewish man who was an American soldier trying to get his parents out of a concentration camp in Germany. The parents of Jack had sent him to America before the invasion of Bon Bon in Germany.[107]

According to Hubert F. Dickey, a World War II veteran and close friend of Hanse "Jack' Hauser, explained this amazing story and why Hanse wrote to Mrs. Roosevelt asking for her help:

> "Hansen 'Jack' Hauser was sent to America before the city of Bon Bon was invaded and people were put into concentration camps. After being in America for quite some time and joining the Army in 1940, Hanse wrote to Mrs. Roosevelt asking for her help to get his parents sent to America. Once Jack's parents received their passport, they would wait to hear any news of joining their son in America.

> When Mrs. Roosevelt received Jack's letter, she signed the
> document in the White House that permitted immigrants to
> board the next ship to America. Sadly, before the people and
> Jack's parents could board the ship, the French invaded many
> cities throughout Germany. Hanse never knew his parents
> were not coming to America until later. His parents died at the
> concentration camp."[108]

This was a very sad and disappointing story about the death of Jack's
parents and the empathy that Mrs. Roosevelt had for all humankind. She
went to great lengths to help people, especially during the Nazi regime.[109]

During the interview, Mr. Dickey never revealed the name of the
concentration camp; the memories were too horrid for him to mention.
Although there is no picture of Mr. Hauser, Mr. Dickey served with him
during World War II in the Army (1939-1945). The stories that he would
tell was heart wrenching and sad. Hanse told this story to Mr. Dickey before
the liberation of the concentration camp that Mr. Dickey kept quiet about,
in Germany.[110] Mr. Dickey has since passed away as of August 2009.

Eleanor Roosevelt never met many of the people she helped throughout
her life although she did help other people in person. Many letters came
addressed to Mrs. Roosevelt at the White House during the years 1933-1945
and she did her best to read every one of them.

A woman with so much energy and enthusiasm to help every single
soul that she could reach out to in every possible way, is so amazing that
when one reads about her most intimate details about each person that she
helped and the reason why she did, is moving beyond words.

Soldiers

Her career in the Social Services and it helped her husband Franklin
since he could no longer walk to do the job himself.

> "In 1943 the President sent his wife as his representative to the
> Pacific front to visit hospitals and encourage servicemen who felt
> neglected because they were not fighting in the front lines."[111]

> In 1943, Eleanor traveled to " . . . several South Pacific areas,
> including Australia and New Zealand, to visit wounded soldiers.
> At first, most of the hardened military officers did not want to

bother with a visit from the First Lady. But at each stop, she charmed everyone she met. The soldiers' eyes lit up when she spoke to them."[112]

Eleanor joined the Red Cross to do the job her husband could no longer perform physically. With Eleanor being herself, the job seemed much easier for people that just seeing her as the President's wife.[113]

"Wearing a Red Cross uniform and traveling in military planes, she covered 23,000 miles by air and stopped in seventeen islands. Overriding her husband's instructions, she insisted on visiting Guadalcanal; she felt that otherwise she could be unable to face soldiers who had been wounded or lost their friends there."[114]

"The morning that Eleanor landed on Guadalcanal, they had breakfast with the "commanding officer."[115] "After breakfast the First Lady began a grueling visit to the island hospitals. In the past few weeks she had talked to thousands of soldiers. And yet she retained an ability to treat each new patient as if he were the first wounded man she had seen." [116]

She traveled to almost every country in the world, visiting military hospitals at every opportunity. She would visit with every service man in the hospital, asking without hesitation if they were getting the very best of care and what else she could get for them.[117]

Eleanor managed to get through what anyone would call horror, when she saw the injured men lying there in the hospital beds.[118]

She constantly urged Franklin that things must change. One of the problems had to do with racial segregation within the military. Some African-Americans could join, but not fight. Nevertheless, she had done many things throughout times of war to help women get jobs in defense and she helped the African-Americans who wanted to join the military and fight for their country. Here is a few key situations in which Eleanor fought so hard to do:

" . . . (2) She played a key role in convincing FDR to establish the Fair Employment Practices Commission, which outlawed racial discrimination in industries that received federal contracts, urged equal treatment for blacks in the military, and helped to ensure that black units, such as the Tuskegee Airmen, had the opportunity to engage in combat . . ."[119]

The soldiers saw her as their friend.[120] Eleanor always wore her Red Cross uniform wherever she traveled in the Pacific.[121] After she had visited seventeen islands, she would then go back to Washington D.C. and gave a full descriptive report to the Red Cross and her husband, then President of the United States, about what she saw, heard, felt, smelled, and witnessed.[122]

As such, Franklin was in no condition to travel and from his time as governor of New York and on, Eleanor became his eyes and ears of the world.[123] Many of the things that she did for the soldiers, which is astounding because of the little things she did that made it possible to get the Red cross to "Americanize" the food they ate.[124]

She was concerned for all the soldiers, black and white, who were serving in the Pacific and abroad.[125] Having clubs and colored people that came there were not as highly educated as she found that the colored soldiers were intimidated by their own class that had more education than they did.[126] She found a balance that suited everyone; however, there is still racism and segregation that went on in the military at that time.

To see how important her travels to the soldiers became through the Red Cross and at the request of the President:

> " . . . She is a great morale builder and charmed everyone by her sincerity and utter simplicity. She arrived on the island at two in the morning and was up and ready to go at six . . . The officers of the hospital and ambulatory patients were gathered out in front when she arrived. She insisted on meeting each of us officers. She then spoke to the entire group. After that she went through practically every ward, stopping to speak with every soldier patient . . . she wanted to know what was wrong with each patient, how they were progressing, and asked them where they were from and in what campaign they had participated, and so on . . ."[127]

Eleanor really cared for these men and encouraged women to do the same. Keeping the economy going while the men were at war (women working in the factories) was another idea that she firmly pressed into the minds of all Americans. She truly wanted world-peace and knew that in order for peace to happen; a lot of hard work on both sides of the table would be needed for it to happen. The first stop to world-peace was to help the soldiers overseas. Letting them know that we, as Americans supported them and would do all that we could to win the war so they could come home again.

The Handicapped

One main reason Eleanor Roosevelt became interested in helping the handicapped, started when her husband Franklin became ill with polio in 1921.[128] It was the hardest time of life from that moment on (1921-1945).

Talking about Eleanor and her work with the handicapped cannot be done without mentioning and extraordinary man who has done astonishing things throughout his life. One man in particular comes to mind and his name is Henry Viscardi.[129]

In A Woman of Quality, there is a great description of Henry when he was born and shows that he would have future struggles due to his severe disability:

> "Henry Viscardi, Jr., was born on May 10, 1912. The second child and only son of an immigrant Italian barber and his wife, he was born with underdeveloped legs" . . . "arrested development of the lower limbs resulting in incomplete growth of the bones and spasticity of the immature, ill-formed muscles."[130]

It would be hard for any person who still had both of their legs to imagine this man as a little boy, growing up with no legs and how people treated him all his life. Eventually, Henry got a pair of artificial legs that he used for many years until he could no longer use them. Henry went back to his doctor to see what he needed to keep walking.[131] He went to see "George Dorsch," another Doctor who deals in prosthetics.[132] Once this was done and he was ready for his new legs:

> "It took many weeks until the aluminum legs were completed. Finally the day came. At twenty-five, Henry saw himself in a mirror-long last a man. He was five feet eight inches tall. He had to learn how to walk, though. At first it was as if he stood on stilts, stilts it would be impossible to manipulate. There was the

dead weight that had to be hoisted from a chair, muscles to be trained, balance to be learned . . ."[133]

This changed his whole outlook on life, himself and the world around him:

> "His sister taught him how to dance. He began going out with girls. He bought a boat and went sailing on the Sound (Puget)."[134] Just to hear how a man who received new legs, finds himself in the world that he had dreamed of being in for so long. He wanted to be in that world working at a job that paid him a decent salary and be to be a completely independent person, not a person on welfare or at the pity of strangers.[135]

When Japan hit Pearl Harbor (December 7, 1941), "Henry Viscardi offered his services to his country. "But what can you do?" The authorities asked.[136] "There is something I can do better than anyone else," replied Henry Viscardi. "I can teach men who lose their legs how to walk again."[137]

Every branch of the service turned him away. " . . . The Red Cross interviewer shook his head" and replied, "We can't give you a job doing physical therapy with amputees. That requires skill and special training. But we might possibly use you in our Field Services."[138]

He has finally done something no other disabled person before him accomplished:

> " . . . now received the rank and pay of an Army captain. He was put on duty at Walter Reed hospital in Washington to work with amputees.[139] After he was asked to see "Dr. Howard Rusk, who headed the Air Force's convalescent Training Division,"[140] He gave a report on Walter Reed Hospital and what he saw. This included anything that was wrong or that the services or that the services and patients lacked in care.[141]

In his report, he mentioned:

> " . . . that the hospital was poorly equipped to meet the great volume of amputees. The prosthetic shop was tiny and totally inadequate. The limb maker wanted to build a cart for a man who

needed legs. The legs the patients did get after an unconscionably long period of waiting were usually so poorly constructed that they often broke the first time they were used."[142]

Henry had the pleasure of meeting Eleanor when she requested he come to the White House for tea.[143] Here she talked to him about what he was doing and became extremely interested. She wondered what she could do to help.[144] There was one thing that she could do for him, help him get in to talk with the industry about changing the things he saw at Walter Reed and giving the handicapped " . . . a chance to make a new life for themselves, to work in order to regain their self-respect . . ."[145]

At this point, everything went smoothly and things began to change over time with the expansion of the hospital and new limb services.[146] "The National Research Council set up a committee to work on the improvement of artificial limbs. This was the beginning of a program that today provides disabled soldiers with the finest prosthetic appliances the world has ever known."[147]

After offering Henry a new job, he talked with Eleanor about it. He knew she was the one person he could count on about this particular subject.[148] Eleanor had ways of telling people that they were special and smart. In Henry's case, she knew exactly what to tell him, "This position is something I feel you are particularly well suited for, with your personal background and your experience. But I think it is you who must make the final decision." [149] Henry already knew this, but he needed that extra support behind him as he moved forward with his life and a new job. This was nothing new that he did not already know.[150]

This new job meant everything to Henry, he would once again, be with those whose disabilities became much more than just losing one or two legs. This company, called Just One Break, helps those who have varying degrees of handicaps get an education and jobs.[151] These people want to be hard-working citizens and taxpayers, not the other way around.

With his new job, he soon became troubled, as there were too many people to help and not enough resources or jobs available:

> "Too many people who came to Just One Break seeking help had to be turned down because of the severity of their disabilities. With four men he set about to find an opportunity for them to work. They set up shop in an unfurnished garage with only five good arms and one good leg among them. They called

the company "Abilities, Inc.," for they were certain that their abilities outweighed their disabilities. The company grew into today's modern, streamlined Human Resources Center . . . where four hundred and fifty "unemployable" workers are running a factory, where handicapped and retarded [developmentally delayed or mentally challenged] children are being taught from pre-kindergarten through high school.[152]

Another reason why Eleanor helped the handicapped was because believed everyone deserved to have a life worth living, even if that meant working a job that was fitted around the disability of that person. For the hearing impaired, she too was enamored at how much the deaf accomplish, even if they were born deaf, mute or both.[153]

Among her many friends, Helen Keller was a close friend. Eleanor would also refer people to Henry Viscardi, as she did with Esther.[154] A woman born blind and later in her life, she went deaf.[155] She wrote to Eleanor asking for her help.[156] She was an educated woman and wanted nothing more than to work and earn money, not become a welfare or disability recipient.[157] For the most part, Eleanor did all she could to refer those who needed the help and often visited Henry over the years.

For Eleanor, she became hard of hearing later in her years. Here is part of a very long quote that Eleanor said about deaf people:

> " . . . One of the advantages of being deaf is that the loss of one faculty sharpens all the others and gives you the perceptions that many hearing people might not have. The only difficult thing is that so many people thing there is something the matter with our mind because it takes you a little while to get accustomed to the way they talk; to be looked upon as a moron when you are extra bright and extra disciplined must take a lot of patience."[158]

African-Americans and Change

People know that African-Americans were slaves in the South and in various parts of the United States for many years. Today, because of the Civil Rights movement of 1955 to 1968, great changes came for thousands and people voiced their opinions of what is right and wrong about the color of a person's skin and equality. One of these people was Eleanor Roosevelt; although she would not see the movement before her death in 1962.

However, "Long before the Civil Rights issue moved to the forefront of the nation's consciousness, she was there, earning public abuse for her quiet reminders of inequalities practiced [in] our land."[159] In 1936, Eleanor made a speech before the "National Urban League" confronting the problems we see every day.[160] These problems hurt the African-American people because of racism.

> " . . . I believe, of course, that for our own good in this country, the Negro race as a whole must improve its standards of living, and become both economically and intellectually of higher caliber. The fact that the colored people, not only in the South, but in the North as well, have been economically at a low level, has meant that they have also been physically and intellectually at a low level. Economic conditions are responsible for poor health in children. And the fact that tuberculosis and pneumonia and many other diseases have taken a heavier toll amongst our colored groups can be attributed primarily to economic conditions. It is undoubtedly true that with an improvement in economic conditions it will still be necessary not only to improve our educational conditions for children, but to pay special attention to adult education along the lines of better living. For you cannot expect people to change overnight, when they have had poor conditions, and adjust themselves to all that we expect of people living as they should live today throughout our country . . ."[161]

In a small section of her speech, Eleanor takes a hard look at the idea that people should not be held back in anything that the person desires to do, regardless of their sex, religion, or skin color. She was determined to change the minds of the world to accept what problems there are, whether in our country or abroad, that as a country whom many look to for assistance, should take a stand to wipe out oppression and step into acceptance.[162]

Another look at what Eleanor accepted as a part of life made her change her views about various organizations in which she had affiliation. One of these organizations shocked her when they denied a famous opera singer, Marion Anderson, the right to sing at Constitutional Hall in 1939.[163] The organization is called "Daughters of the Revolution."[164] Eleanor accepted people for who they were, not for their skin color, religion, or sex, and soon other people followed her, believing this discrimination again Marion Anderson to sing is detestable.

> "The New York Times, . . . declared: "If Miss Anderson's inability to find a suitable hall in the national capital for her April concert is due to social or racial snobbery, all that can be said is that such an attitude is inconsistent with the best American traditions, including those which were born in the fires of the American Revolution. It is hard to believe that any patriotic American organization in this country would prove of discrimination against so gifted an artist could so and still merit the adjective patriotic."[165]

Eleanor gave her opinion, or at the very least, voiced her beliefs whenever she became aware that someone or groups of people are hurt by racial oppression and or segregation. In the case of Marion Anderson:

> "Eleanor Roosevelt, however, as was her custom, did more than protest; she took action."[166] In her column, "My Day," on February 27, 1939:

> "I have been debating in my mind for some time, a question which I have had to debate with myself once or twice before in my life. Usually I have decided differently from the way I am deciding now. The question is, if you belong to an organization and disapprove of an action which is typical of a policy, should you resign or is it better to work for a changed point of view within the organization? In the past, when I was able to work actively in any organization to which I belonged, I have usually stayed until I had at least made a fight and been defeated.

> Even then, I have, as a rule, accepted my defeat and decided I was wrong or perhaps, a little too far ahead of the thinking of the majority at that time. I have often found that the thing in which I was interested was done some years later. But, in this case, I belong to an organization in which I can do no active work. They have taken an action which has been widely talked

of in the press. To remain as a member implies approval of that action, therefore I am resigning."[167]

This is astonishing in many respects. Eleanor tells people that if you belong to an organization that does not fall in line with your beliefs, such as hers, then it is wise to leave that organization. Marion Anderson did give her concert; however, it was at another monument in Washington, the Lincoln Memorial on April 9, 1939.[168] Eleanor did not just publicly voice her growing frustrations with segregation; she showed her interest in wiping this atrocity out by doing what is right. One story told by Dr. Robinson,[169] mentions that:

> "Mrs. Roosevelt participated in our group," . . . "Several Negroes from New York and elsewhere had gone to Washington and they had no place to go for lunch since the restaurants in the neighborhood refused to service them. When we brought the situation to Mrs. Roosevelt's attention, she listened attentively, [and] then she said, 'Very well, we'll all eat together in the lobby.' She arranged for a large urn of coffee and sandwiches every day at noon, and set up folding chairs in the lobby of the Du Pont Building to serve her and all the workers on the committee. Luncheon with Mrs. Roosevelt in the lobby became so popular that the restaurants in the building felt a sharp drop in their business and decided to lift their restriction."[170]

It does not take a genius to see that Eleanor could make a change without opening her mouth and give a big speech on how anyone or any business restricting African-Americans the right to buy or use any facility. She cared only that the workers worked just as hard as she did; they deserved to eat the same food as the white people and had the right to choose where they ate.[171]

The pressing matter man people realize or know of during the Civil Rights movement (1955-1968), began long before Martin Luther King, Jr. Many followers during the fifties and sixties that Eleanor fought for, way before she became the First Lady of the White House, would follow her in her beliefs. One of the most amazing women that Eleanor had the pleasure of knowing was Mary McLeod Bethune (1875-1955).[172] She had lived a remarkable life.

Some of the things that Mary did was, open a school for African-American (1904), and " . . . in 1935 she founded the National Council of Negro Women, which united the major black women's associations nationally, and served as the council's president until 1949."[173]

> "She became the first African-American woman to be a presidential adviser when Franklin Roosevelt named her director of Negro Affairs of the National Youth Administration in 1936. In addition, she served as special adviser to FDR on minority affairs. She created the federal Council on Negro Affairs, a group of African-Americans working to strengthen black support of FDR's New Deal, to decrease discrimination, and to increase the number of government jobs for black Americans . . . She served as Vice-President of the NAACP from 1940 to 1945, and later became Vice-President of the National Urban League."[174]

The National Council of the Youth Congress Affiliations helped to get the bill passed for the American Youth Act (1935-1937).[175]

> "This was a youth-employment relief bill introduced a the request of the Youth Congress, a measure which we conceded would cost $3.5 billion, and which critics said would cost fifteen to twenty billion dollars."[176] "The Youth Act was our answer to the National Youth administration which President Roosevelt had established six months earlier to provide employment for needy young people. We did not know it then, but the idea for a National Youth Administration had come from Mrs. Roosevelt."[177]

Mrs. Roosevelt tried to help get the Anti-Lynching bill passed, so that African-Americans would no longer be subjected to this kind of physical torture and mental or emotional abuse.[178]

However, this bill has been introduced and brought before the congress and House of Representatives and the Senate since 1918. The bill passed through Congress and the House, but it was blocked by the Senate each time. Then in the fifties and sixties, this bill was again brought forth as the Civil Rights Movement gained momentum. Again, it was passed by Congress and the House, but blocked by the Senate. This bill would not come up again until 2005 when it was passed by the government in the hopes that their apology for not protecting the rights of the African-Americans all this time (over a hundred years), could now be laid to rest.

Women and Work during the Depression

The Depression Era (1929-1942) was a time of high unemployment and despair for many people in America. When men who could not get work, the women did their best to help bring in money and tried to feed their families. Some of these jobs came in the form of sewing, cleaning, and cooking.

One fact not known about Eleanor Roosevelt is she would put on interviews for only women at the White House.[179] "Eleanor Roosevelt would have regular press conferences, but only women reporters would be allowed in."

> "Hick [Lorena Hickok] had suggested that Eleanor hold press conferences and, after clearing it with Franklin and Louis, she held her first, limiting it to women reporters so as to encourage the papers to employ more women. The women assembled in the Red Room and she came in, outwardly serene, inwardly atremble. She had been brought up to avoid the press."[180]

These women knew they had Eleanor to thank for their jobs, and became very protective of the First Lady.[181] She supported the reporters who wanted to cover her speeches on the United Nations, Women's Rights, Civil Rights, our youth, and their education.[182] People were very interested as one newspaper reporter remembers.[183]

> "[Marcia Levy who was a college senior in 1956 and her boss at the newspaper wanted her to crash the dinner party that Mrs. Roosevelt was attending].[184] She intended to do so, until she found Mrs. Roosevelt lying down for a quick nap in one of the rooms upstairs.[185] Marcia accidentally awoke Mrs. Roosevelt and apologized for waking her up.[186] She explained why she was there and Mrs. Roosevelt accepted to give her a full interview."[187]

Like so many other press conferences that she held at the White House, she had only let women in during the time of the Depression and World War II, when many people lost their jobs.[188] Men on the other hand, could get some kind of job anywhere. Women, sadly enough, were extremely limited in skills outside the home. These female reporters came every week for a new story; having to keep their jobs so that they could keep on supporting their families.[189]

On the other hand, there was another side to the Depression Era. Young boys and girls who came into the adult world after high school, found it to be rather repressive and scary.[190] When the Depression hit, people had no idea what to do, where to go, how to feed their families, pay their rent or mortgages, and more importantly, if they would be able to keep their jobs.

> "The first task of the Roosevelt administration was to meet the urgent need for relief. People needed to eat; they had to find jobs . . . letters pleading for help came pouring in to Mrs. Roosevelt. Her deep concern was instantly aroused and, as always, she responded to every appeal that came to her. Now, thirty-five years later, many people still remember her attempts to help them."[191]

> "The years of the Depression were especially hard and bewildering for America's young people who were just emerging into the adult world after high school. Many felt that they were a burden to their families, sensing that by their very presence they were taking food away from their younger brothers and sisters. There was no place for them in the labor market. Letters pleading for help came pouring in to Mrs. Roosevelt, and she took a very special interest in these unfortunate youngsters. She immediately devoted her time to various programs of the American Friends Service Committee and the government Civilian Conservation Corps which inaugurated voluntary work camps for young people"[192]

A memory from a woman who spent time at one of these encampments for young people:

> " . . . My family had to go on welfare and my brother worked for the WPA," wrote Freeda Menschel of Arverne, Long Island. "I was promised a job by the government but, until one materialized, I was sent to Camp Jane Addams, a camp for jobless and homeless

girls, which was sponsored by Mrs. Roosevelt and which she often visited."[193] " . . . What I felt was so very special about Mrs. Roosevelt was that she didn't just go around making speeches; she truly did help so many people by doing so many wonderful things." [194]

"Freeda Menschel is one of the many young people who were given a chance for a better life during the Depression through the efforts of Eleanor Roosevelt. The idea of the work camps outlived the days of the Depression. In 1939 it took the form of the Work Camps for Democracy. In 1940 and 1941, this citizenship training program expanded under the name of "Work Camps for America," and, in the years following World War II, the program evolved into its present form—"The Encampment for Citizenship"-an undertaking in which Eleanor Roosevelt was vitally interested."[195]

In the camps that Eleanor and Franklin started, she managed to go there and see how the developments were coming along and how the people were doing. She would eat the same food the people were eating, she sat on the same chairs or benches that the people sat on, and no one felt less than human in her presence. One could accept as truth, that Eleanor always managed to bring a little bit of peace and hope everywhere she went. She had a lot of ingenuity, creativity, and passion for helping people and they felt that passion within her everywhere she went.

3

The Jews and Israel

Eleanor Roosevelt cared for the plight of the Jews until her death in 1962. However, she did not always feel this way. At one point, Eleanor had asked a friend why the Jews are the way they are and this is the response from the book, *A Woman of Quality*. Which Hershan reveals as told to Eleanor:

> "Judge Polier told Mrs. Roosevelt that while the hurts of the Jews in America were not physical, their lives were still shadowed. While free superficially here, the Jews are not truly free because they live in a hostile world."[196]

It was her concern for the inner freedom of all people that made Eleanor Roosevelt remarked in one of her speeches that,

> "the promotion of better understanding among Protestants, Catholics, and Jews in America is truly one of the most necessary tasks confronting us, not only for the sake of lasting, social peace and goodwill, but in order that the idealism of religion may make its most effective contribution to the welfare of the Nation. None of our children should grow up without respect for every other American citizen, but when you have schoolbooks that don't tell you what each different group has contributed to the making of the country, it is very hard for children to understand what they have in riches of heritage."[197]

"Her sympathy for the persecuted, her sense of justice, and her respect for the struggle of the Jews to reestablish their own identity in their own homeland, led her to respond wholeheartedly to the creation of the State of Israel . . ."[198]

Eleanor believed that if the nations came together, including the United States, to help those Jews whose annihilation by Hitler and those who managed to escape, still had nowhere to go. Many countries allowed the Jews to stay in their country with a visa and for a certain amount of time. Having nowhere to go, Eleanor pushed as hard as she could and urged the President (Truman) and his cabinet members, to do what is right.[199]

This is Eleanor's belief as she tried to help the Jews outside the government:

"Mrs. Roosevelt spoke, raised funds, and gave whatever support she could to the embattled people of Israel. It is not because they are Jewish people only . . . It is because they are a people building a nation which will be valuable to the world. Americans should support Israel because that country will someday spread Democracy throughout the Near East."[200]

The whole idea behind helping the Jews, developing Israel, and for the Jews to have a place they can call home, was a huge turning point in Eleanor's belief in the fundamental rights of all people everywhere. To highlight this, there are a few passages from the book, *A Woman of Quality*, that the author, Hershnan, shows how Eleanor got her start:

" . . . Mrs. Roosevelt, she had very little knowledge of the land that was to become Israel. It was shortly after end of World War II. There was a long discussion on whether the people in the Displaced Persons Camps in Germany should have the right to choose whether they could or would return to their countries of origin. The Soviet Union insisted that anyone who did not want to do that was either a "Quisling" or a traitor, and the committee argued the question for weeks. To Eleanor Roosevelt it seemed to be a question of fundamental human rights. She approached the United States Ambassador and asked him if she could go to Germany and see the camps they had been talking about for herself . . ."[201]

"We landed first at Frankfurt . . . where there were a number of refugee camps, including one for Jew in Zilcheim. I was greeted by leaders of the Jewish refugee group. They had built a small hill with steps leading to the top where they had erected a stone monument inscribed: 'To the memory of all Jews who died in Germany.' In all the Jewish camps there were signs of the terrible events through which these people had passed and of the hardships they continued to suffer. In the mud of Zilcheim I remember an old woman whose family had been driven from home by war and madness and brutality. I had no idea who she was and we could not speak each other's language. But she knelt in the muddy road and threw her arms around my knees. 'Israel . . . Israel! Israel!' As I looked at her weather beaten face and heard her old voice . . . I knew for the first time what that small land meant to so many, many people."[202]

After her visit to Israel in 1959, Eleanor tells of her experience:

"There is an atmosphere in Israel that one does not find in many other countries . . . Its young people are partly responsible for it. They are excited by the dream of building a country; they are willing to work with their full youthful energy to achieve unbelievable results. They have imagination they know how to handle people, and they have plenty of experience in adjusting themselves to the handling of people of different background, different religions and different customs.

The United Jewish Appeal has been the principal instrument through which money has been collected for work in this country and for work in Israel. I believe that a country in which deserts have been reclaimed and where, despite a tremendous influx of immigrants, the standards of health have been raised and education is provided for the majority of the people . . . whatever is done is Israel will serve in the long run to help stabilize an area of the world that needs peace for its future development. A strong and Democratic Israel can mean a strong and Democratic Middle East, and for that reason I am willing and anxious to help the UJA."[203]

One way in which Eleanor believed that she could help was to join the United Jewish Appeal in 1952.[204]

"In 1952, Mrs. Roosevelt agreed to become the World Patron of Youth Aliyah . . . Youth Aliyah is an organization for the rescue and rehabilitation in Israel of homeless children throughout the world. It originated in Nazi Germany to save Jewish children in danger of extermination, and became the greatest child rescue movement in history. Today in Israel, one citizen in every twenty was once a Youth Aliyah child."[205]

There were countless numbers of people in Israel, at least in terms of generations, who came from this organization that helped numerous children when the Nazi began extermination of all Jews. One can clearly see that a child is more likely to live through their time in the concentration camp than an adult whose health was failing from medical problems or old age.

Looking at the adults today, the way people eat, has a huge effect on our bodies before we reach adulthood. After we reach physical maturity (adulthood), the damage done over the years since childhood, gives the adult in a concentration camp, a likely chance of not surviving. Albeit, each individual is different and no two people are alike in that make up. To read about scores of children, now adults in Israel who survived incarceration in the camps and continue to carry with them the memories of their experiences that brought them to the land they now call 'home.'

"Mrs. Roosevelt immediately expressed her desire to see the work of Youth Aliyah, and, when she visited Israel a few months later . . . she was deeply interested in the developments that had taken place and she seized every possible opportunity to meet those responsible for the education of the children to see for herself how the children were educated and cared for . . . Mrs. Roosevelt stated at the end of her tour that, to her mind, the most important and greatest need of Israel was the integration of tis youth into a united people, and not, as she had previously thought, its economic independence."[206]

"Eleanor Roosevelt . . . viewed her patronage as an important role in her public life and never once gave a negative answer to any of our requests. She traveled widely for Youth Aliyah in Great Britain, France, Canada, and Mexico. She participated actively in the Hadassah Conventions as well as those of other Women's Zionist organizations in the United States of America and accepted many speaking engagements for Youth Aliyah. She visited the Youth Aliyah camp at Cambus near Montpellier in the south of France, where she asked to meet with children from Morocco."[207]

"Recognition of Youth Aliyah rose enormously on hearing what she had to say about this humanitarianism and educational project. She came to France on a youth Aliyah mission, and visited first of all the Youth Aliyah transition camp at Cambus near Montpellier in the South of France. She met children who had come from Morocco and other countries of North Africa, and who were being treated for ringworm, trachoma, and vitamin deficiencies."[208]

One of her speeches on what the Jews, Israel, and America really meant to her:

"We in America at present stand before the world as their great hope for future peace and understanding among nations. Here in our land of many races and many religions have lived side by side. They have learned something far better than tolerance. Tolerance implies a certain condescension. There should be no element of condescension between one American citizen and another American citizen. We have learned to treat people as individuals and to give them their due, regardless of race, religion, or background.

You may say that this is not always in actuality and that of course is true, but in the great documents to which the aspirations of the people of the United States are recorded you will find that discrimination on racial or religious grounds is always openly eschewed . . . And down through the history of our country Jewish people have held their place. They have fought wars; they have given us geniuses in the fields of art and literature and scientific development, to our entertainment and our sports, they have contributed to our economic success. The Jews are part of the life of our nation. What the United States is today does not belong to any one of the racial and religious groups any more than it does to the Jewish group. They make up a comparatively small percentage of our population, but their contribution is in some cases out of proportion to their numbers . . ."[209]

Lash gives an insight to what Eleanor tried to do away from the public view by using some of her political influence:

"She did what she could to open America's doors to the survivors of the Holocaust, having little sympathy with the extreme Zionist position that Palestine was the only place where Jews might live in safety and without apology. I fear Palestine could never support all the Jews, and the Arabs would start a constant war if all of them came . . ."[210]

However:

"On the basis of the British pledge, endorsed by Woodrow Wilson, and their agreements with the Arabs, the Jews had brought hundreds of thousands of settlers to Palestine and transformed the arid deserts into garden spots,"[211]

With all the problems with the Arabs not wanting the Jewish people in Palestine and then the land divided into two, which gave the Jews the state of Israel, caused many problems. Nevertheless, only one country wanted the Jews to come and they had plenty of land. According to author, Joseph Lash, from his book, *Eleanor: The Years Alone,*

"Dr. Milton Steinberg, who was described to her as neither Zionist nor anti-Zionist and who brought her a plan for Jewish resettlement in Australia, which needed people and had an overabundance of land that could easily be developed. She thought enough of this plan to forward it immediately to her husband at Warm Springs . . . The immediate issue was what to do with the homeless and destitute Jews coming out of the extermination camps."[212]

" . . . I cannot bear to think of the Jews of Europe who have spent so many years in concentration camps, behind wire again on Cyprus. Somehow it seems to me that the 100,000 Jews should be let into Palestine and that some real agreement should be reached with the Arabs."[213]

"In May, 1949, Israel was voted a member of the United Nations. The day the flag of Israel was added to all the other flags outside of the UN area at Lake Success was a memorable one: There was a lump in almost everybody's throat, I think, at the thought of a new nation being born and one whose people had suffered greatly . . ."[214]

Human dignity and perseverance through what the Jews have suffered since Hitler, is justifiable in giving the Jews something that they could be proud to call their own. Since the acceptance of Israel, they have been able to protect themselves from other enemies and still to this day, struggle with being free with their own beliefs and religion.

4

Labor Unions

She Tried to Make Life Better

Early in her life (after 1902), Eleanor became interested in the Labor Unions. While attending some of the union meetings, any of the women [Marion Dickerman and Nancy Cook] sought her out because she was interested in what was going on in the world and that change is coming. Eleanor joined the union in 1922 [Women's Trade Union League] and stayed with them until her death in 1962.[215]

> "Long before Eleanor Roosevelt was the First Lady, even before she was married to Franklin Delano Roosevelt, she came down to the lower East Side of New York to work in a settlement house on Rivington Street. And thus, she came to know the sweatshop, the home industries of women and small children sewing buttons on pants making paper flowers, earning a penny here and there; falling asleep at the table, falling off a bench, many children crowded in one room."[216]

> " ... She had met many of its leaders at the International Congress of Working Women, which had been held in Washington at the end of 1919. Now she pitched into the League's efforts to raise money for a clubhouse."[217]

> "Eleanor Roosevelt then went to work with Florence Kelley of the Women's Trade Union League which was battling for equal

pay for equal work, for protection for pregnant women who had to work under horrible conditions for a livelihood . . . She devoted herself to rectifying the faults which appeared in our society."[218]

"From 1907 through 1922, the WTUL achieved a number of its legislative goals, including an eight-hour workday, a minimum wage, and the abolition of child labor. After the 1911 fire at the Triangle Shirtwaist Company factory, the WTUL took part in a four-year investigation that ultimately helped establish new industrial safety regulations. In addition, the league helped women gain access to labor unions, trained women for leadership positions within unions, and even provided temporary assistance for unemployed trade union women."[219]

"Eleanor was aware of the importance of the unions as early as 1934."[220] One of the incidents that Eleanor had witnessed was the Triangle Fire of 1911.[221] "These men, women, and children who had worked for a pittance in the factory sweatshops which had signs that said, 'If you don't come in Sunday, don't bother to come in Monday.' I thought of the girls who had worked at the sweatshop of the Triangle Shirtwaist Company and finally leaped to their deaths in that fire, women who had to pay for the thread they needed in their work by selling their young bodies."[222]

How horrible for men, women, and children, to suffer such atrocities just to make a penny. In cases such as this one, one of many incidents, the working conditions for them were ghastly, as they had no heating for the winter, no fresh air at all, and the long working hours to the point of exhaustion, is enough for any of the to get seriously hurt at their job.

Making worker's pay for the things that they need to do their job is utterly wrong. Once they pay for their stuff and if anything breaks, then they pay for that too. After that, the worker has no money to buy food, pay rent or buy clothes for his or her family.

"They [the union] strongly believe in such things as health insurance, a minimum-wage law, and an end to child labor."[223] Members of the WTUL also joined strikes, or refusals to work, by female workers in the garment industry in order to obtain better working conditions."[224]

Labor Unions marched for all kinds of reasons. One of these reasons being wages or working conditions went on time after time in New York City. Whenever there was one, Eleanor always heard about them and she was there to lend her support. How long these protests were did not matter to Eleanor. She stayed for as long as it took or at least until she had to leave.[225]

One of the most important unions was the " . . . Amalgamated Clothing Workers of America which represents the workers in the men's clothing industry."[226] The president of this company, "Mr. Potofsky" supported all the charities that Eleanor gave her time in helping.[227] He helped as much as he could; donating money to her causes.[228]

> "Despite the league's closeness to the White House during the Roosevelt years, the WTUL's role grew increasingly irrelevant once labor unions allowed women to join on a widespread basis. Mounting financial problems and declining membership numbers also hampered WTUL's effectiveness. Even though ER remained supportive of the League until the end, the WTUL closed its doors for good in 1950."[229]

> "Let us make the dream world that all of us want, not a dream world, but a reality, a practical reality brought about by a nation that understands what living Democracy means . . . I think it is essential to our nation's leadership that we convince the peoples of the world that color and race have nothing to with our interest in the family of man."[230]

The League of Women Voters gave Eleanor a willingness to help others in another way other than settlements. Most of the labor unions that Eleanor joined were to fight for women's rights, among other problems [wages] within society and businesses.

> "Her settlement house experience led to her enrollment in the National Consumers' League, headed by Florence Kelley, a group devoted to improving conditions for women who worked in factories. It had an activist agenda and operated by means of

> a 'white list' that named the retail establishments which dealt
> 'justly' with their employees and which the League's members
> and friends were urged to patronize." (2) Practices that would
> justify gaining a positive recommendation included equal pay
> for equal work, a minimum wage, a ten our day, and exclusion
> of child labor, particularly in sweatshops.
>
> ER worked on the committee that monitored compliance with
> the standards. Hesitant at first, she saw firsthand the misery
> of the sweatshop. (3) From that time forward she was firmly
> committed to social justice. But her view of how to achieve
> that justice began with the reformers, and so her sense of what
> gave people an equal stake in society derived from those initial
> experiences."[231]

Eleanor not only went to some of the strikes or dealt with the politics
of the unions without Franklin, she urged women that the need for women
in politics is necessary. With Franklin, however, she regularly talked with
him about appointing women in political offices. Some of the women
whom Franklin appointed are Mary Mcleod Bethune and Miss Perkins
" . . . who became the first cabinet member."[232] These two women among
many others set the precedence for women later on.

Finding information on the League of Women Voters and Eleanor
Roosevelt has its challenges. From several resources, not much is there as to
exactly what Eleanor did for them. From the understanding of the league,
the union supports women and tries to get women into politics and to
vote. Voting is an important part of politics that helps people to decide
what issues are necessary for change.

For example, when people decided to vote on the Nineteenth
Amendment, it became a huge and vital change for women in general.
When women entered politics, it not only involved what the men thought,
but the women thought of other issues within society that needed change
and some men had never gave credence to or simply ignored those issues.

> " . . . She [Eleanor] agreed to serve as Vice-President of the
> New York state branch of the League of Women Voters. The
> League was the successor of the National American Woman
> Suffrage Association . . . Franklin encouraged her to work for
> the League, and when she brought him problems that had come

up in her legislative committee enjoyed the role of tutor . . . Both political parties had begun to be concerned with the women's vote. Eleanor, the niece of Theodore and the wife of Franklin, knew that politics was where power rested-but in tandem with, not opposition to, the men, as she indicated to Franklin from Cleveland, where she attended the League's second national convention as Dutchess Country delegate."[233]

"As part of the process of getting to know the League, she had made friends of Esther and Elisabeth. She spent one evening a week with them at the Greenwich Village apartment reading French literature, something she had not done since the days of Mlle. Souvestre. They admired her insistence on doing her own work and not trading on her name."[234]

"They were among a number of pairs of women, most of whom lived in the Village, most of them veterans of the suffrage battles . . . These veterans of the suffrage wars played a considerable role in the education of Eleanor Roosevelt. They ran many of the movements that shaped the thinking of the Twenties and kept alive many of the programs that flowered into the New Deal."[235]

"Her reasons for being in politics, however, were not that she was a forty-year old woman with empty hours to fill, or that she was the surrogate for a crippled husband. She had her own vision of a better world and was attracted to the people who shared that vision."[236]

Anyone looking at the history of Eleanor Roosevelt would find that she felt a strong need to change the world and make it a better place. This change included the disadvantaged and abused children, African-Americans, women, immigrants and refugees, and the handicapped. This included the access to education, voting rights, protection for refugees, working conditions, decent working wages to support a family, and health insurance; among her many charities and interests that she lobbied for.

Eleanor was a feminist in her own right, although some see her as just a woman poking around in the business of others. She was a woman who grew up wealthy, disadvantaged as a child, and able to connect with the problems of the world in which she tried to change.

5

The United Nations

Changing the World, One Document at a Time

After the death of her husband, the President, Franklin Roosevelt, Truman took the seat as President since Roosevelt died before his term was over. Then in 1945 then President, Harry S. Truman, asked Eleanor Roosevelt to sit on the board of the United Nations that her husband, FDR and started.[237] This committee formed for reasons of ensuring that all people have equal rights throughout the world.

However, Eleanor Roosevelt would find opposition from many scholars and politicians alike.[238] Unbeknownst to them, she was an experienced speaker and politician.[239]Voicing what she believed to be right and wrong in giving all people, whether foreign or domestic, the right to be free and this is what the *Declaration of Independence* says: " . . . the right to life, liberty, and the pursuit of happiness . . ."[240] Eleanor set a goal to make this idea of equality happen.[241]

A committee [Committee III], in which she worked with, would be the most difficult project in her life until her death in 1962. There are representatives from every country [58 in all] and each country voiced their opinion of what they wanted or would accept.[242]

Eleanor knew this and found that many countries would not accept the idea of equal rights worldwide.[243]

> "In 1961, JFK asked her to lead his commission on the status of women. The group studied unfair treatment of women in jobs and society."[244]

"Eleanor lived another seventeen years after Franklin and in that time established herself as an international diplomatic figure. President Truman appointed her a delegate to the first meeting of the United Nations in London in December 1945. Here, she again displayed her political acumen, staring down the delegate from the Soviet Union [the U.S.S.R.] on the important issue of human rights."[245]

"Working eighteen hour days she negotiated and moderated until a document was drafted that would define human rights. It passed unanimously on December 10, 1948, and Eleanor received a standing ovation."[246]

"Many of us thought that lack of standards for human rights the world over was one of the greatest causes of friction among the nations, and that recognition of human rights might become one of the cornerstones of which peace could eventually be based."[247]

"The members of the Commission were made government representatives, chosen by the Economic and Social Council . . . At present the following are represented on the commission: Australia, Belgium, Byelorussia, China, Chile, Egypt, France, India, Lebanon, panama, the Philippines, Ukraine, the U.S.S.R., Jugoslavia, Uruguay, the United Kingdom and the United States."[248] "The first session of the full Commission was called in January 1947."[249] "The drafting committee then men in June 1947 . . ."[250]

Upon reading about the various countries, big and small, they each had their own reasons to which they agreed or disagreed in voting for the declaration.[251] Yet, the representative or delegate from the Union of Soviet Social Republic would make it difficult to come to a complete agreement on the subject of human rights.[252] Various people realize that the Declaration of Human Rights is not a legal or binding piece of paper. However, many nations have discussed this document during long hours as to what it means to be free and have the right as a human being to live.[253] Just to give you an idea why Eleanor accepted to work on Committee III and why the other representatives worked so hard on this Declaration, here are a few lines from each page of the document:

"No one shall be held in slavery or servitude; slavery and the slave trade shall be prohibited in all their forms."[254]

"No one shall be subjected to torture or to cruel, inhuman or degrading treatment or punishment."[255]

"(1) Everyone charged with a penal offence has the right to be presumed innocent until proved guilty according to law in a public trial at which he has had all the guarantees necessary for his defense."[256]

These first three passages chosen, is interesting as we all know that before the nineteen-sixties, slavery was a widely accepted practice for the use of African-Americans. Eleanor did not approve of such behavior, although in the upper wealthy classes of society it was a common practice to have a black man as a butler or a black woman as a maid. Nevertheless, slavery was outlawed in the United States, but it is still practiced in other countries. The next quote is used in the legalities of our judicial system.

All the different sections of the *Declaration of Human Rights*, if looked at carefully, is separated into areas of interest to the committee and can be closely associated with the *Declaration of Independence* and *the Bill of Rights*. The next few quotes will show the protection of the family, nationality, the right to see refuge in any country, and property.[257]

"(1) Everyone has the right to seek and to enjoy in other countries asylum from persecution."[258]

"(2) This right may not be invoked in the case of prosecutions genuinely arising from non-political crimes or from acts contrary to the purposes and principles of the United Nations."[259]

"(1) Everyone has the right to a nationality."[260]

"(2) Marriage shall be entered into only with the free and full consent of the intending spouses."[261]

"(3) The family is the natural and fundamental group unit of society and is entitled to protection by society and the State."[262]

"(1) Everyone has the right to own property alone as well as in association with others."[263]

The key idea here is that everyone in the world is entitled to pursue what makes them happy and free. We as a people were born with free will and Eleanor understood this concept, which is why she included the 'free and full consent' from the passage, cited above. It used to be a common practice in many countries, that when girls and boys grew to a certain age and sometimes at birth, that they were 'promised' to another later in life.

Many times over, this practice lasted for hundreds of years and many generations into the future. Albeit, there would be times that a person who had to enter into an arranged marriage that allowed the fusion of two families for purposes of political or non-political reasons, was common.

Eleanor Roosevelt disapproved of such a practice, as it was during her early life that the Victorian Era practiced such a ritual. This occurred mainly within the upper wealthy classes for political reasons and society status. Other times, it was not so much an arranged or promised marriage but a marriage within the same blood line to protect the sanctity of the family name, money, social status, and to keep the blood line pure, which sometimes resulted horribly in genetic disorders.

The next section deals with work, government, "social security," and "freedom of expression."[264]

"(1) Everyone has the right to freedom of peaceful assembly association."[265]

"(1) Everyone has the right to take part in the government of his country, directly or through freely chosen representatives."[266]

"(2) Everyone has the right to equal access to public service in this country."[267]

"(1) Everyone has the right to work, to free choice of employment, to just and favorable conditions of work and to protection against unemployment."[268]

"(2) Everyone, without discrimination, has the right to equal pay for equal work."[269]

One of the main things that Eleanor believed is entitlement to work, security, and education. The next section deals with education, sources of materials, and their community.[270]

> "(1) Everyone has the right to education. Education shall be free, at least in the elementary and fundamental stages. Elementary education shall be compulsory. Technical and professional education shall be made generally available and higher education shall be equally accessible to all on the basis of merit."[271]

> "(3) Parents have a prior right to choose the kind of education that shall be given to their children."[272]

> "(1) Everyone has the right to freely participate in the cultural life of the community, to enjoy the arts and to share in scientific advancement and its benefits."[273]

> "(2) Everyone has the right to the protection of the moral and material interests resulting from any scientific, literary or artistic production of which he [or she] is the author."[274]

> "Eleanor served in the United Nations until 1953."[275]

This document [*Declaration of Human Rights*] is closely related to the *Bill of Rights*, the *Declaration of Independence* and the *Constitution*. She [Eleanor] seemed to be so patriotic toward this country, our government, and the people, who she wanted to, make a change in society; in order for people to want that change, it was necessary that all humans feel free to make those choices without reprimand, taunting, belittling, or downright abuse of one person or group to another.

The freedom to their education is their right and anyone who uses materials (sources) for purposes of writing papers, learning, and or writing a book, for example, must give credit to the author or authors.[276] As mentioned before, this paper is not a legal binding paper, only which is of a moral and ethical obligation to treat one another with compassion, humility, kindness, and the understanding that everyone is no different in the fact of being born.[277]

Everyone has something different and unique about him or her and that is what makes everyone special. Each nation wanted this document to be in every language in the world and for many countries, the wording of this document must be right. To say that 'all men' just in the *Declaration of Independence* or *Constitution*, for many women in many countries, suggests that women are not included in this right with men. Therefore, dealing with the wording was difficult at first.

Eleanor saw everything from the slums of the poor to the wealthy and their 'household slaves,' to the horrors of wounded soldiers and the concentration camps. She understood the fundamental need to belong and to be heard, without anyone being condescending to them or restricting what they are allowed to do because you are a woman, African-American, a Jewish person, a poor person, or other prejudices of her time.

The *Declaration of Human Rights,* accepted by all delegates except for one country. On December 10, 1948, everyone voted unanimously, except for the U.S.S.R. This was a huge victory for Eleanor as she became the victor in a long struggle of the many horrors, tragedies, and solemn things she has witnessed, felt, dealt with in her marriage, and over came as a child whose parents (both mother and father) died before she was eleven years old. Every person has the right to read it, understand it, and question it.

6

Conclusion

A Life Lived with Purpose and Dignity

Eleanor Roosevelt lived a life full of broken promises, heartbreak, emotional and mental abuse, adventure, a marriage turned political partnership, and a purpose that was not apparent to her until late in her years. This purpose was to promote the fundamental rights of all people, all classes, and all religions, as well as the right to education. At the center of this purpose became the women, children, immigrants, refugees, and the African-Americans.

She was a formidable politician in the eyes of the people. Her husband, FDR, was a good politician, on the other hand, he at least came to the realization sometime after his affair with Lucy Mercer affected his marriage, that what he could not do she did better. Eleanor walks into a room full of politicians (Democrats) with the room in a complete uproar and she never had to open her mouth for people to stop and listen to what she had to say.[278] If she had not helped her husband fight for the Vice-Presidency, they would have gone to the White House where she was able to use her husband and his seat of power to further her causes.

Eleanor Roosevelt worked on all her charities through her life, until she died on November 10, 1962. Helping refugees, immigrants, women and children, giving children a place to grow up and get a decent education; she fought for Civil Rights, no matter the skin color, sex, religion, or creed. She believed in equality. As the author, I have never known a woman whom many have such a high regard and admiration for, would inspire so many people to fight for what is right.

Whether a response came in the form of a letter, a phone call, or simply, a personal visit, she was always a woman with a smile of gold and a heart full of love. She never complained during hard times, times of war, times of heartbreak, disaster or illness, but jumped in with both feet and did what she could. Traveling the world over, she tried to make the world a better place to live and help those who served our country.

Thus, the unconditional love Mrs. Roosevelt gave to people the world over showed her constant connection with people. Despite her background, she pushed for rights, equality, education, housing, and employment and always treated people with the greatest respect.

.

APPENDIX A

Illustrations

Her life in Pictures

Her Early Life

Fig. 1 Eleanor with her Father and siblings
From www.yahoo.com

Fig. 2 A very young Eleanor
From www.yahoo.com

Fig. 3 Eleanor Roosevelt at eighteen
From www.yahoo.com

Fig. 4 Eleanor on her wedding way March 17, 1905 [279]
From www.yahoo.com

Fig. 5 Eleanor with her mother-in-law, Sara Roosevelt
From www.yahoo.com

Fig.6 Eleanor with young Franklin
From www.yahoo.com

Fig 7 Eleanor as an older adult
From www.yahoo.com

Fig. 8 Eleanor and Madame Chiang Kai Shek
From www.yahoo.com

Fig. 9 A poster when Eleanor flew with Amelia Earhart
From www.yahoo.com

Fig. 10 Eleanor with Mary Mcleod Bethune
From www.yahoo.com

Fig. 11 Eleanor and Marion Anderson
From www.yahoo.com

Fig. 12 Eleanor with the Red Cross
From www.yahoo.com

Fig. 13 Eleanor at the United Nations
From www.yahoo.com

Fig. 14 Eleanor holds the Declaration of Human Rights
From www.yahoo.com

Fig. 15 The grave of Eleanor and Franklin at Hyde Park, NY
From www.yahoo.com

Notes

1. Allison, Lassieur *Eleanor Roosevelt: Activist for Social Change.* (Canada: Franklin Watts, 2007), 17.
2. Joseph P. Lash and Franklin Delano Roosevelt Jr. *Eleanor and Franklin.* (New York: W.W. Norton and Company, 1971), 80.
3. Ibid., 19-21.
4. Ibid., 19-21.
5. Ibid., 17-21.
6. Ibid., 21.
7. Lash and Roosevelt Jr., *Eleanor and Franklin*, 97-99.
8. Ibid., 97-99.
9. Tamara K. Hareven. *An American Conscience,* (Chicago: Quadrangle Books, 1968), 10-11.
10. Ibid., 10-11.
11. Ibid., 64-65
12. Lassieur, *Eleanor Roosevelt: Activist for Social Change,* 64-65.
13. Hershnan, *A Woman of Quality,* 168-173.
14. Ibid., 168-173.
15. Ibid., 20-33.
16. Ibid., 22.
17. Ibid., 29-30.
18. Lassieur, *Eleanor Roosevelt: Activist for Social Change,* 84-85.
19. Public Broadcasting Service, 1999. April 06, 2010.
20. Hareven, *An American Conscience,* 145-161.
21. Ibid., 145-161.
22. Ibid., 90-103.
23. Ibid., 90-103.
24. Ibid., 90-103.

25. Ibid., 156.

26. Ibid., 156.

27. Ibid., 63-73.

28. Ibid., 123-137.

29. Ibid., 123-137.

30. Ibid., 123-137.

31. Ibid., 123-137.

32. Ibid., 176-183.

33. Eleanor Roosevelt, *My Day.*

34. Lash and Roosevelt Jr., *The Years Alone.* 36.

35. Ibid., 19-37.

36. Lassieur, *Eleanor Roosevelt: Activist for Social Change,* 10.

37. James Roosevelt. *My Parents: A Differing View.* (Chicago: Playboy Press Book, 1976), 11.

38. Rachel A, Koestler-Grack. *The Story of Eleanor Roosevelt.* (New York: Chelsea House Publishers, 2004), 6.

39. Lash and Roosevelt Jr., *Eleanor and Franklin,* 44.

40. Ibid., 39.

41. Ibid., 44.

42. Lassieur, *Eleanor Roosevelt: Activist for Social Change,* 13.

43. Lash and Roosevelt Jr., *Eleanor and Franklin,* 58.

44. Ibid., 91-94.

45. Ibid., 75.

46. Ibid., 75.

47. Ibid., 75.

48. Ibid., 80.

49. Ibid., 80-84.

50. Ibid., 75.

51. Ibid., 75.

52. Lassieur, *Eleanor Roosevelt: Activist for Social Change,* 20-21.

53. Lash and Roosevelt Jr., *Eleanor and Franklin,* 84-85.

54. William T. Young *Eleanor Roosevelt: A Personal and Public Life.* (Boston: Little, Brown and Company, 1985), 63.

55. Lash and Roosevelt Jr., *Eleanor and Franklin,* 85.

56. Ibid., 85.

57. Ibid., 87.

58. Lassieur, *Eleanor Roosevelt: Activist for Social Change,* 21.

59. Ibid., 21.

60. Lash and Roosevelt Jr., *Eleanor and Franklin,* 87.

61. Ibid., 98.

62. Ibid., 97.

63. Ibid., 98.

64. Ibid., 98.

65. Ibid., 97-98.

66. Ibid., 98.

67. Lassieur, *Eleanor Roosevelt: Activist for Social Change,* 54-57.

68. Ibid., 56.

69. Virginia Veeder Westervelt. *Here Comes Eleanor.* (Greensboro: Avisson Press, 1998), 50.

70. Lash and Roosevelt Jr., *Eleanor and Franklin,* 56.

71. Lassieur, *Eleanor Roosevelt: Activist for Social Change,* 57.

72. Ibid., 57.

73. Westervelt, *Here Comes Eleanor,* 50.

74. Joseph P. Lash, *Love, Eleanor, Eleanor Roosevelt and Her Friends.* (Garden City: Double Day and Company, 1982), 110.

75. Westervelt, *Here Comes Eleanor,* 71.

76. Hershnan, *A Woman of Quality,* 20-24.

77. Ibid., 21-23.

78. Ibid., 22.

79. Ibid., 21-25.

80. Ibid., 20-33.

81. Ibid., 20-33.

82. Ibid., 20-33.

83. Ibid., 20-33.

84. Ibid., 20-33.

85. Ibid., 20-33.

86. Ibid., 26-27.

87. Ibid., 29.

88. Ibid., 25-29.

89. Ibid., 28-30.

90. Ibid., 28-30.

91. Ibid., 28-30.

92. Ibid., 31-32.

93. Ibid., 32.

94. Ibid., 30-31.

95. Ibid., 20-32.

96. Ibid., 33-47.

97. Ibid., 33-47.

98. Ibid., 35.

99. Ibid., 35.

100. Ibid., 45-47.

101. Ibid., 45-47.

102. Ibid., 46.

103. Ibid., 46.

104. Ibid., 46-47.

105. Ibid., 47.

106. Ibid., 33-47.

107. Dickey. Hubert F. Mr. Crystal P Roberts. August 2007.

108. Ibid.

109. Ibid.

110. Ibid.

111. Hareven, *An American Conscience,* 156.

112.

113. Hareven, *An American Conscience,* 145-161.

114. Ibid., 157.

115. Eleanor Roosevelt. *This I Remember.* (New York: Harper and Brothers, 1949), 307.

116. Young, *Eleanor Roosevelt: A Personal and Public Life,* 9.

117. Hareven, *An American Conscience,* 145-161.

118. Ibid., 145-161.

119. Allida Black. "What did Eleanor do during World War II?" Eleanor Roosevelt National Historic Site, http://www.nps.gov/archive/elro/who-is-er/q-and-a/q21.htm.

120. Hareven, *An American Conscience,* 145-161.

121. Ibid., 145-161.

122. Lash and Roosevelt Jr., *Eleanor and Franklin,* 364-365.

123. Lassieur, *Eleanor Roosevelt: Activist for Social Change,* 62-63.

124. Hareven, *An American Conscience,* 155.

125. Ibid., 158-159.

126. Ibid., 158-159.

127. Ibid., 158.

128. Hershnan, *A Woman of Quality,* 90.

129. Ibid., 90.

130. Ibid., 94.

131. Ibid., 96.

132. Ibid., 96.

133. Ibid., 96.

134. Ibid., 96.
135. Ibid., 96.
136. Ibid., 97.
137. Ibid., 97.
138. Ibid., 97.
139. Ibid., 97.
140. Ibid., 97.
141. Ibid., 97.
142. Ibid., 97.
143. Ibid., 97.
144. Ibid., 98.
145. Ibid., 98.
146. Ibid., 98.
147. Ibid., 98.
148. Ibid., 100.
149. Ibid., 100.
150. Ibid., 100.
152. Ibid., 101.
153. Ibid., 103.
154. Ibid., 93.
155. Ibid., 93.
156. Ibid., 93.
157. Ibid., 93.
158. Ibid., 103.
159. Ibid., 155.
160. Anna Eleanor Roosevelt, "Eleanor's Legacy, "http://www.eleanorslegacy. com/about/eleanor_roosevelt/speeches/the_negro_and_social_change/.
161. Ibid.
162. Ibid.
163. Hershnan, *A Woman of Quality*, 156.
164. Ibid., 156.
165. Ibid., 156.
166. Ibid., 157.
167. Ibid., 157.
168. Ibid., 166.
169. Ibid., 166.
170. Ibid., 166.
171. Deborah G. Felder. *The 100 Most Influential Women of All Time-A Ranking Past and Present.* (New York: Carol Publishing Group, 1996), 151-154.

172. Ibid., 152-153.

173. Ibid., 153.

174. Joseph P.Lash. *Eleanor Roosevelt: A Friend's Memoir. A Close-up View of The First Lady.* (Garden City: Double Day and Company, Inc., 1964), 3.

175. Ibid., 3.

176. Ibid., 3.

177. Ibid., 40.

178. Lassieur, *Eleanor Roosevelt: Activist for Social Change,* 70.

179. Lash, *Love, Eleanor, Eleanor Roosevelt and Her Friends,* 136.

180. Lassieur, *Eleanor Roosevelt: Activist for Social Change,* 70.

181. Hershnan, *A Woman of Quality,* 63-73.

182. Ibid., 63-73.

183. 65-66.

184. 65-66.

185. Ibid., 65-66.

186. Ibid., 65-66.

187. Ibid., 63-73.

188. Ibid., 63-73.

189. Ibid., 168-175.

190. Ibid., 169.

191. Ibid., 170.

192. Ibid., 170.

193. Ibid., 171.

194. Ibid., 171.

195. Ibid., 123.

196. Ibid., 123-124.

197. Ibid., 124.

198. Ibid., 123-137.

199. Ibid., 124.

200. Ibid., 124-125.

201. Ibid., 125.

202. Ibid., 128.

203. Ibid., 128.

204. Ibid., 129.

205. Ibid., 129.

206. Ibid., 130.

207. Ibid., 131.

208. Ibid., 135.

209. Lash and Roosevelt Jr., *The Years Alone,* 109.

210. Ibid., 111.

211. Ibid., 112-113.

212. Ibid., 118.

213. Ibid., 137.

214. National Historic Site/Eleanor Roosevelt. *Eleanor Roosevelt National Historic Site.* April 06, 2004, http://www.nps.gov/archive/elro/glossary/womens-trade-union-league.htm.

215. Hershnan, *A Woman of Quality,* 177.

216. Lash, *Love, Eleanor, Eleanor Roosevelt and Her Friends,* 82.

217. Hershnan, *A Woman of Quality,* 177.

218. National Historic Site/Eleanor Roosevelt. *Eleanor Roosevelt National Historic Site.* http://www.nps.gov/archive/elro/glossary/womens-trade-union-le182.ague.htm.

219. Hershnan, *A Woman of Quality,* 182.

220. Ibid., 176.

221. Ibid., 183.

222. Lassieur, *Eleanor Roosevelt: Activist for Social Change.* 47.

223. Ibid., 53.

224. Hershnan, *A Woman of Quality,* 176-184.

225. Ibid., 180.

226. Ibid., 180.

227. Ibid., 180.

228. National Historic Site/Eleanor Roosevelt. Eleanor Roosevelt National Historic Site. http://www.nps.gov/archive/elro/glossary/womens-trade-union-le182.ague.htm.

229. Hershnan, *A Woman of Quality,*181.

230. Susan Abrams Beck. "Eleanor Roosevelt: The Path to Equality," *US History,* April 11, 2010, 1-4, http:///www.find.galegroup.com.

231. Judy Klemesrud. "Assessing Eleanor Roosevelt as a Feminist." *New York Times,* November 5, 1984, Sec. B.

232. Lash, *Eleanor, Eleanor Roosevelt and Her Friends,* 80.

233. Ibid., 81-82.

234. Ibid., 82.

235. Ibid., 104.

236. Lash and Roosevelt Jr. *The Years Alone,* 36.

237. Ibid., 36-37.

238. 38-81.

239. Thomas Jefferson. "Declaration of Independence." *US History,* July 4, 1995. http://www.UShistory.org.,1.

240. Lash and Roosevelt Jr. The Years Alone, 38-81.

241. Ibid., 38-81.

242. Ibid., 38-81.

243.

244. Maggie Reichers. "National Endowment For the Humanities." April 14, 2010. http://www.neh.gov/new/humanities/2000-01/eleanor.html, 4.

245. Ibid., 4-5.

246. Allida Black. "The Promise of Human Rights." *Universal Declaration of Human Rights Organization*, April 14, 2010. http://www.udhr.org/history/amerview.htm, 2.

247. Ibid., 2.

248. Ibid., 2.

249. Ibid., 2.

250. Ibid., 1-6.

251. Ibid., 1-6.

252. Nations, General Assembly of the United. "Universal Declaration of Human Rights." *Universal Declaration of Human Rights*, (Sorrbonne, France: United Nations, December 10, 1948), 1-6.

253. Ibid., 2.

254. Ibid., 2.

255. Ibid., 3.

256. Ibid., 3-4.

257. Ibid., 3.

258. Ibid., 3.

259. Ibid., 3.

260. Ibid., 3.

261. Ibid., 3.

262. Ibid., 4.

263. Ibid., 4.

264. Ibid., 4.

265. Ibid., 4.

266. Ibid., 4.

267. Ibid., 4.

268. Ibid., 4.

269. Ibid., 5.

270. Ibid., 5.

271. Ibid., 5.

272. Ibid., 5.

273. Ibid., 5.

274. Koestler-Grack, *The Story of Eleanor Roosevelt,* 26.

275. Nations, 5.

276. Ibid., 1-6.

277. Lash and Roosevelt Jr., *The Years Alone,* 70.

Bibliography

Beck, Susan Abrams. "Eleanor Roosevelt: The Path to Equality." *US History*, April 11, 2010. http:///www.find.galegroup.com.

Black, Allida. "The Promise of Human Rights." *Universal Declaration of Human Rights Organization*, April 14, 2010. http://www.udhr.org/history/amerview.htm.

-Black, Allida. "Eleanor Roosevelt: The Courage To Lead, Social Activist, Party Lead, First Lady, Journalist, Diplomat." *Eleanor's Legacy*, January 23, 2010. http://www.eleanorslegacy.com/eleanor_roosevelt/bio.

-Black, Allida. "What did Eleanor do during World War II?" *Eleanor Roosevelt National Historic Site,* April 06, 2010. http://www.nps.gov/archive/elro/who-is-er/q-and-a/q21.htm.

Dickey. Hubert F. Mr. Crystal P Roberts. August 2007.

Eleanor Roosevelt. By Sue Williams. Dir. Sue Williams. Warner Home Video. Prod. Katherine Dietz. 2000

Felder, Deborah G. *"The 100 Most Influential Wome of All Time-A Ranking Past and Present."* New York: Carol Publishing Group, 1996. 151-154.

Hareven, Tamara K. *An American Conscience.* Chicago: Quadrangle Books, 1968.

Hershnan, Stella. *A Woman of Quality.* New York: Crown Publishers, 1970.

Jefferson, Thomas. "Declaration of Independence." *US History,* July 4, 1995. http://www.UShistory.org.

Kaplan, Richard. Producer. *The Eleanor Roosevelt Story.* Kino Intern Corporation, 1965.

Klemesrud, Judy. "Assessing Eleanor Roosevelt as a Feminist." *New York Times*, November 5, 1984, Sec. B12.

Koestler-Grack, Rachel A. *The Story of Eleanor Roosevelt.* New York: Chelsea House Publishers, 2004.

Kulling, Monica. *Eleanor Everywhere: The Life of Eleanor Roosevelt.* New York: Random House, 1999.

Lash, Joseph P. and Franklin Delano Roosevelt Jr. *Eleanor and Franklin.* New York: W.W. Norton and Company, Inc., 1971.

Lash, Joseph P. *Eleanor Roosevelt: A Friend's Memoir. A Close-up View of The First Lady.* Garden City: Double Day and Company, Inc., 1964.

—. *The Years Alone.* New York: W.W. Norton & Company, 1972.

—. *Love, Eleanor, Eleanor Roosevelt and Her Friends.* Garden City: Double Day and Company, Inc., 1982.
Lassieur, Allison. *Eleanor Roosevelt: Activist for Social Change.* Canada: Franklin Watts, Imprint of scholastic, Inc., 2007.

McClure, Ruth and Dorothy Dow. *Eleanor Roosevelt An Eager Spirit. Selected Letters of Dorothy Dow*, New York: W.W. Norton and Company, 1984.

National Historic Site/Eleanor Roosevelt. *Eleanor Roosevelt National Historic Site.* April 06, 2004. http://www.nps.gov/archive/elro/glossary/womens-trade-union-league.htm.

Nations, General Assembly of the United. "Universal Declaration of Human Rights." *Universal Declaration of Human Rights,* Sorrbonne, France: United Nations, December 10, 1948.

Reichers, Maggie. *National Endownment For the Humanities.* April 14, 2010. http://www.neh.gov/new/humanities/2000-01/eleanor.html.

Roosevelt, Anna Eleanor. "Eleanor's Legacy". January 23, 2010, http://www.eleanorslegacy.com/about/eleanor_roosevelt/speeches/the_negro_and_social _change/.

Roosevelt, Curtis. *Too Close To The Sun.* New York: Public Affairs, 2008.

Roosevelt, Eleanor *This I Remember.* New York: Harper & Brothers, 1949.

—. *My Day.* April 06, 2010. http://www.gwu.edu/~erpapers/myday/

Roosevelt, Elliot and James Brough. *The Roosevelts of Hyde Park: An Untold Story.* New York: G.P. Putnam's Sons, 1973.

—. *The Roosevelt's of The White House, A Rendevous With Destiny.* New York: G.P. Putnam's and Son's, 1975.

Roosevelt, James. *My Parents: A Differing View.* Chicago: Playboy Press Book, 1976.

Shop. Picture Print History. Yahoo. April 14, 2010. http://www.yahoo.com/images.

Westervelt, Virginia Veeder. *Here Comes Eleanor.* Greensboro: Avisson Press, Inc., 1998.

Yahoo images, April 14, 2010. http://www.yahoo.com/images.

Young, Williams. *Eleanor Roosevelt: A Personal and Public Life.* Boston: Little, Brown and Company, 1985.

Index

CPSIA information can be obtained at www.ICGtesting.com
Printed in the USA
BVOW02s1003060715

407555BV00001B/64/P